3 1994 01454 7514

1/12

SANTA ANA PUBLIC LIBRARY

D0742169

To

_____

_____

From

_____

_____

Written and compiled by Sophie Piper
Illustrations copyright © 2010 Giuliano Ferri
This edition copyright © 2010 Lion Hudson

The moral rights of the author and illustrator
have been asserted

A Lion Children's Book
an imprint of
Lion Hudson plc
Wilkinson House, Jordan Hill Road,
Oxford OX2 8DR, England
www.lionhudson.com
ISBN 978 0 7459 6135 4

First edition 2010
10 9 8 7 6 5 4 3 2 1 0

All rights reserved

Acknowledgments
All unattributed prayers are by Sophie Piper and
Lois Rock, copyright © Lion Hudson.

The Bible extracts on the back cover (from
Matthew 5:9) and pages 6, 27, 42, 43, and
45 are taken or adapted from the Good News
Bible, published by The Bible Societies/
HarperCollins Publishers Ltd, UK ©
American Bible Society 1966, 1971, 1976,
1992, used by permission.

Prayer by Mother Teresa (page 16) used by
permission.

A catalogue record for this book is available
from the British Library

Typeset in 15/18 Caslon Old Face BT
Printed in China July 2010
(manufacturer LH06)

Distributed by:
UK: Marston Book Services Ltd, PO Box 269,
Abingdon, Oxon OX14 4YN
USA: Trafalgar Square Publishing,
814 N Franklin Street, Chicago, IL 60610
USA Christian Market: Kregel Publications,
PO Box 2607, Grand Rapids, MI 49501

Peace on Earth

Poems and Prayers for Peace

J 242.62 PIP
Piper, Sophie
Peace on earth

CENTRAL $9.99
                    31994014547514

Written and compiled by Sophie Piper

Illustrated by Giuliano Ferri

LION
CHILDREN'S

O God,
Settle the quarrels among the nations.

May they hammer their swords into ploughs
and their spears into pruning knives.

From the book of Micah, chapter 4, in the Bible

Contents

8

One world

We share the earth
we share the sky
we share the shining sea
with those we trust
with those we fear:
we are God's family.

Points of view

May we learn to appreciate different points of view:

to know that the view from the hill is different from
    the view in the valley;
the view to the east is different from the view
    to the west;
the view in the morning is different from the view
    in the evening;
the view of a parent is different from the view
    of a child;
the view of a friend is different from the view
    of a stranger;
the view of humankind is different from the view
    of God.

May we all learn to see what is good, what is true,
what is worthwhile.

Our shared journey

I am a pilgrim
on a journey
to the place
where God is found;
every step
along that journey
is upon
God's holy ground.

O God,
We are all strangers in this world
and we are all travelling to your country.

So may we not treat anyone as a foreigner or an
  outsider,
but simply as a fellow human being
made in your image.

Courage

In the face of evil and wrongdoing
I will surely not be happy,
Nor will I let myself grow too sad.
Instead, I will choose to stand up for what is right
And I will face the future
With calm and courage and cheerfulness.

Hold on to what you believe in
Even if it is a tree that stands by itself.

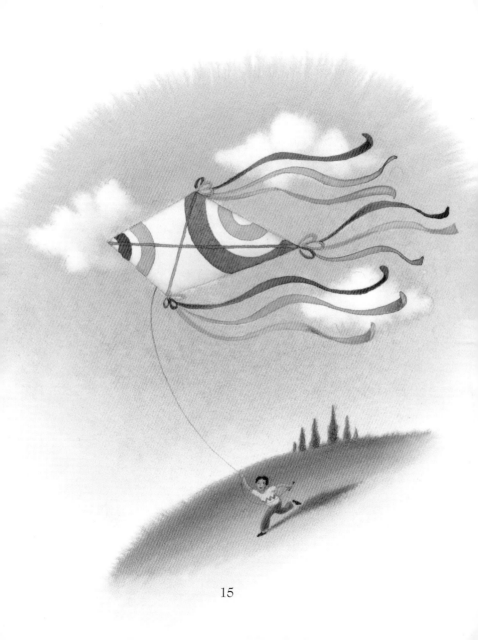

15

Love

Love is giving, not taking,
mending, not breaking,
trusting, believing,
never deceiving,
patiently bearing
and faithfully sharing
each joy, every sorrow,
today and tomorrow.

Anonymous

We can do no great things,
Only small things with great love.

Mother Teresa of Calcutta (1910–97)

What to do
in a war

When all the talk is of the war,
sing a song of peace.

When all the view is of the ruins,
dream a dream of peace.

When enemies are all around,
share the bread of peace.

Ask the important question

"We must make war," said the government.
"We know that this war is just."
What can be fair about bombing homes
and turning them all to dust?

"We can make war," said the government,
"without shedding too much blood."
So why are there bodies, cold and grey,
lying face down in the mud?

"We won the war," said the government,
"and now we'll enforce the peace."
So why do they keep their guns in place?
Why are no prisoners released?

"We must make war," said the government,
"to bring all wars to an end."
But how can a war stop the fighting?
How can a war make us friends?

21

Say a prayer

Dear God,
We pray for the casualties of war:

for the young and the old,
for the parents and the children;

for the birds and the animals,
for the fields and the flowers;

for the earth and the water,
for the sea and the sky.

We pray for their healing.

Lord, watch over refugees,
their tired feet aching.
Help them bear their heavy loads,
their bent backs breaking.
May they find a place of rest,
no fears awake them.
May you always be their guide:
never forsake them.

Forgive

Dear God,
Give us the courage to overcome anger with love.

How can the angry world ever find peace?
When will the gentle years start?
I have no answer, but I pray that God
will let peace grow strong in my heart.

From the mud
a pure white flower

From the storm
a clear blue sky

As we pardon
one another

God forgives us
from on high.

Love your enemies

This is what Jesus says:

"You all know this saying, 'Love your friends, hate your enemies.' But now I am telling you something different: love your enemies and pray for those who deliberately hurt you."

Words of Jesus from the Gospel of Matthew, chapter 5, in the Bible

We pray for the people who are condemned as wicked: those who are responsible for wars and massacres and terrorism.

We pray that people of good faith will find a way to stop them.

We also pray that you and we will treat them with justice and mercy.

Peace

Peace for the seed
and peace for the flower,
peace for each sunlit
golden hour.

Peace for the garden,
peace for the field,
peace for the harvest's
golden yield.

Peace for a season,
peace for a year,
peace for a lifetime –
world without fear.

Make me an instrument of your peace

Lord, make me an instrument of your peace.
Where there is hatred, let me sow love;
Where there is injury, pardon;
Where there is discord, union;
Where there is doubt, faith;
Where there is despair, hope;
Where there is darkness, light;
Where there is sadness, joy.

O divine Master, grant that I may not so
much seek to be consoled as to console, to
be understood as to understand, to be loved
as to love; for it is in giving that we receive,
it is in pardoning that we are pardoned, and
it is in dying that we are born to eternal life.

Attributed to St Francis of Assisi (1181–1226)

Making friends

We
not me.

Share
not tear.

Mend
not end

and so
befriend.

O God,
Gather together as one
those who believe in peace.
Gather together as one
those who believe in justice.
Gather together as one
those who believe in love.

Bringing down the wall

Why is there a wall between us –
Wall of concrete, wall of wire,
Wall of deeply rooted hatred,
Wall of angry bullet fire?

On the wall I write a poem:
Words of hope and words of peace;
On your side, you paint a picture
Of the time when war will cease.

On that day, we'll bring you flowers;
You'll bring fruit grown in your land.
We will celebrate together –
Sisters, brothers, hand in hand.

35

Change

May the world turn round about,
may all things turn to right;
may the sunset thank the dawn,
the noontime bless the night;

May the rivers thank the rain,
the stormclouds bless the sea;
may the good soil thank the leaves,
the sunshine bless the tree;

May the rich thank those in need,
the children bless the old;
may the strong thank those who fail,
the timid bless the bold;

May the angels sing on earth,
may heaven hear our prayer;
may forgiveness, joy and peace
and love fill everywhere.

The olive tree

The olive tree I thought was dead
has opened new green leaves instead
and where the landmines tore the earth
now poppies dance with joy and mirth.

The doves build nests, they coo and sigh
beside the fields where corn grows high
and grapes hang heavy on the vine,
and those who fought share bread and wine.

39

40

Trust

When all love is lost from sight,
Wait for dawn and watch for light

Gather memories, gather flowers –
Lovely things for lonely hours.

Slowly, slowly, you will find
Love is patient, love is kind.

Love will wipe away your tears;
Love will last for more than years

Flowers may fade, but love will never.
Heaven's love will last for ever.

The Good Shepherd

This is what God says:

"I myself will look for my people and take care of them in the same way as shepherds take care of their sheep.

"I will bring them back from all the places where they were scattered on that dark, disastrous day.

"I will lead them to the mountains and the streams of their own land, so they may make their home amid the green pastures.

"I shall be their God, their Good Shepherd; they will be my people, my flock."

From the book of Ezekiel, chapter 34, in the Bible

Hope returns when I remember this one thing:
God's unfailing love and mercy still continue,
Fresh as the morning, as sure as the sunrise.

From Lamentations, chapter 3, in the Bible

Sleep in peace

When I lie down, I go to sleep in peace;
you alone, O Lord, keep me perfectly safe.

Psalm 4:8

Deep peace of the running waves to you,
Deep peace of the flowing air to you,
Deep peace of the quiet earth to you,
Deep peace of the shining stars to you,
Deep peace of the shades of night to you,
Moon and stars always giving light to you,
Deep peace of Christ, the Son of Peace, to you.

Traditional Gaelic blessing

Index of first lines